STANDARD COMPANION TO NON-AMERICAN

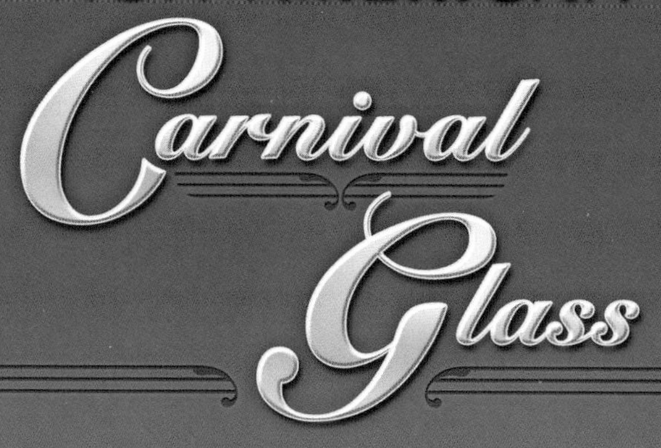

IDENTIFICATION
&
VALUE GUIDE

Bill Edwards

Mike Carwile

COLLECTOR BOOKS

A Division of Schroeder Publishing Co., Inc.

Front Cover:
Rekord (also know as Diamond Wedges) vase, Eda Glass of Sweden, $425.00.

Cover design by Beth Summers

Book design by Allan Ramsey

COLLECTOR BOOKS
P.O. Box 3009
Paducah, Kentucky 42002-3009

www.collectorbooks.com

The current values in this book should be used only as a guide. They are not intended to set prices, which vary from one section of the country to another. Auction prices as well as dealer prices vary greatly and are affected by condition as well as demand. Neither the authors nor the publisher assumes responsibility for any losses that might be incurred as a result of consulting this guide.

Searching for a Publisher?

We are always looking for people knowledgeable within their fields. If you feel that there is a real need for a book on your collectible subject and have a large comprehensive collection, contact Collector Books.

Preface

This edition features carnival glass from around the world, all from non-American companies. As the reader will soon see, the production was vast and not all patterns are shown here.

The format is the same as our *Collector's Companion to Carnival Glass*, showing only vital information of pattern name, maker, date of production, shapes, colors, and current values; this gives an easy-to-carry reference.

Remember this is only a guide and doesn't establish prices, which vary from one location to another depending on condition, rarity, and desirability, but also on quality of iridescence.

Bill Edwards
2245 Shawnee Dr.
Cottage #2
Madison, IN 47250-3748
(812) 265-2940

Mike Carwile
180 Cheyenne Dr.
Lynchburg, VA 24502
email: carwile@centralva.net
mcarwile@jetbroadband.com

NOTE: Unlike American sugars, European sugars are usually open and shaped like small stemmed compotes.

Contents

Introduction

Once an interest by the public for Carnival glass became apparent in America in the early 1900s, it was only a matter of time before other parts of the world began to share this interest.

Through export, glass soon reached England and the continent of Europe, and in the 1920s, factories there began to produce their own designs in this inexpensive iridized glass.

Factories in Sweden, Finland, Denmark, Czechoslovakia, Holland, Mexico, France, Germany, and Argentina are now known to have produced some amount of iridized glass. While it would be impossible for us to catalog all these companies, I will list a few of the more prolific ones and their currently known patterns.

Germany

Since the appearance of the 62-page Brockwitz catalog that was unearthed by Bob Smith, we've been able to piece together a better picture of Carnival glass from Germany. Brockwitz opened in 1903 and the factory was indeed a huge concern with a veritable army of workers. By the late 1920s the factory was the largest in Europe. In addition, we've learned that patterns shown in the Brockwitz catalog were also made by Riihimaki and Karhula of Finland and Eda of Sweden so it is possible Brockwitz sold or transferred some of their moulds to other concerns in Europe. Patterns shown in the Brockwitz catalog include Rose Garden, Curved Star (Cathedral), Moonprint (also thought to have been made in England), Lattice and Leaves, Footed Prism Panels, Sunflower and Diamond, Superstar, Daisy and Cane (Tartan), Diamond Cut Shields, Christ and Maria candlesticks (Saint), Draped Arcs, and Rose Band, as well as the Triple Alliance cookie jar. Colors are primarily marigold or cobalt blue with the glass of a fine quality.

Finland

Carnival glass from Finland has been traced to two factories: Riihimaki Glass and the Karhula-Iittala factory. Riihimaki was established about 1911 or 1912 and began their production of iridized glass in the late 1920s. Patterns include Western Thistle, Grand Thistle, Drapery Variant, Moth (Firefly), Four Flowers, Tiger Lily Variant, Garland and Bows, Tulip and Cord, Starburst, Flashing Stars, Fir Cones, and Column Flower (Square Diamond). Colors are mostly marigold, blue, or amber. The Karhula-Iittala factory began their iridized production about 1932. Their patterns include Diamond Ovals (once believed to be from England), the Britt tumbler, Quilted Fans, and another version of the Curved Star pattern. In addition there appear to be some pieces of Fleur de Lis that are very close to the Inwald pieces. Colors are mostly mairgold or cobalt blue.

Czechoslovakia

We continue to learn more each year about iridized glass production in this region of Europe. The discovery of catalogs by Bob Smith, and more recently Siegmar Geiselberger in Germany, have given us at least a partial list of items produced by Inwald, Rindskopf, and factories around the Gablonz area that made beads, hatpins, buttons, and jewelry. Production was greater than we ever suspected and continued from the early 1900s to the beginning of WWII. In some areas production resumed after the war and continues today.

Sweden

In 1920 five Swedish glassmakers came to America to learn the American process of glassmaking, spending two years at Durand Glass, then moving to Imperial, and later to Fenton. When they returned to Sweden they took the knowledge of iridized glassmaking and shared this knowledge throughout Sweden and Finland. Swedish and Finnish companies had a close relationship, and mould swapping between the two countries was fairly common. In addition, both areas bought and traded moulds with Brockwitz, and iridized glass became a production item well into the 1930s. Colors seem to be marigold or cobalt blue but amber has also been used in Finnish glass.

Holland

Some minor production of iridized glass seems to have occured in the Netherlands by the Leerdam Glass Works. Production is said to date to the 1930s with much of the glass made for export. Patterns include the Meyham design which we show in a covered butter dish (it is also used in a creamer). The coloring of the known pieces is soft marigold, similar in many respects to glass made in England.

France

Little information about iridized glass from France is known, but we do know of pieces that are marked "Made in France" or just "France." We show a small bowl called French Grape and the beautiful Fircone vase. The bowl is a clear iridized piece with a vaseline flashing while the rare vase is in marigold. Future research is bound to turn up more patterns from France and only time will tell us a complete story.

Argentina

Three glass companies produced iridized glass in Argentina: the Cristalerias Rigolleau S.A. (a company founded by Leon Rigolleau in Buenos Aires and maker of both the Beetle ashtray and the CR ashtray); Cristalerias Papini of Buenos Aires; and Cristalerias Piccardo. The companies were all nationalized in the 1940s and only the Rigolleau and Papini companies are still in business. (The latter, now called Cristalux, no longer produces iridized glass). In addition, Argentina imported glass from the U.S., Finland, Sweden, Czechoslovakia, and England. Cristalerias Papini patterns include the Goodyear ashtray, the Industria Argentina Star pattern, as well as some European patterns that include Jacobean, Princeton, and Curved Star. Cristalerias Piccardo patterns include Graceful (aka Fantasia), Band of Roses, and a rare pitcher called Imperial (it has matching goblets and resembles the Octagon pattern). Finally, many patterns of U.S. Glass (The States, Ominbus, and Rising Sun) have shown up in Mexico and South America and are suspect.

Mexico

Glass production in Mexico began in the early 1900s with the Vitro Company of Vidriera, Monterrey, producing glass for beer bottles and continuing with an expansion when American companies began supplying natural gas for glass production in the 1920s. Other companies arose, one of which was Cristales Mexicanos, a producer of household glass and dinnerware. Here, iridized glass seems to have been concentrated and production continued for several years. Patterns include Oklahoma, Ranger, and the Votive Light piece.

Peru

While there has been little documentation from Peru, we know the 9½" bottle called Inca was made there (it bears the lettering: "Huaco de Oro Peruano") and another bottle of the same design is imprinted on the base: "Vina Santa Josefa...Imitation Moderna. SEH...2171."

China

When we first showed the Shanghai tumbler we thought it was perhaps just a one-shot move toward iridized glass from China, but since then, other tumblers including Golden Triangle, Snow Chrysanthemum, and the Etched Vine tumbler have been found. Markings may say "Shanghai," "China," or "Made in China." Most have a #4 on the base. We believe these were all made in the 1930s prior to WWII. In addition, we've been told that some items in iridized glass may have been made in Indonesia, including versions of an iridized Buddha (probably made for export). Obviously we have no proof of this, but we hope future research will give us the facts. Rumors also persist about glass from the Philippines but we have no evidence of any at this time.

India

When we first leaned about products of the Jain Glass Works, we felt we'd covered the subject, but through long correspondence with Vikram Bachhawat, we've learned there were indeed more than 20 glassmakers in India following World War II. Jain was simply one of the prominent ones. Others include Paliwal Glass Works and Agarwal Glass Works. Since we find pieces that are signed AVM and CB, we still have much to learn. Jain was founded in 1928 and at one time employed some 2,500 workers. It closed in 1986.

English Carnival Glass

Once iridized pressed glass became a success in the United States and American makers began to export this product, glassmakers in Britain soon began to look at this product as something they could produce. Sowerby had been in the business of making fine glass since the 1850s and soon rose to the task, producing such patterns as the Sowerby Drape vase, the Diving Dolphin footed bowls, the Daisy Block rowboat, the Covered Swan and Covered Chick (Hen), Pineapple (Pineapple and Bows), Pinwheel, Derby, Wickerwork, Flora, African Shield, Cane and Scroll (Sea Thistle), English Hob and Button (aka Chunky), Lea (and the variants), and Royal Swans. Sowerby also copied the Imperial Scroll Embossed pattern and used it in several ways, including the interior of their Diving Dolphins pieces.

In addition, other smaller glass firms made some limited carnival glass. These include Molineux, Webb of Manchester, Crystal Glass in Knottingley, Yorkshire, the Canning Town Glass Works, Ltd., and Walsh of Birmingham. English Carnival glass began in the 1920s and continued throughout the 1930s with many pieces that equal or exceed U.S. quality. Colors were primarily marigold or cobalt blue, but amethyst, amber, aqua, and green (scarce) are known.

Australian Carnival Glass

The Australian Crystal Glass Company Limited was established in 1914 and was making carnival glass by 1922. Most of the well-known patterns from this company began in 1924 in bowls, compotes, salvers, and vases. The product was mostly press-moulded and the main colors were marigold or purple. However, a bottle green treatment with amber iridescence is known in an Emu bowl and an ice blue with flashed marigold is reported. Patterns known to be from Australia are:

Australian Swan
Banded Diamonds
Blocks and Arches
Bull rush and Orchids
Butterflies and Waratah
Butterfly Bower
Butterfly Bush
Crystal Diamonds
Emu (also called Ostrich)
Feathered Flowers
Flannel Berry
Flannel Flower
Hobnail and Cane
Kangaroo & variants
Kingfisher & variants
Kiwi
Kookaburra & variants
Magpie & variants
Pin Ups
Petals and Cane
S Band (Broken Chain)
Star and Drape
Style
Threads
Thunderbirds (Shrike/Cookoo)
Water Lily & Dragonfly
Wild Fern

Trademarks

Some non-American glassmakers trademarked pieces just as some American makers did. Below is a sampling of just what the collector may expect to find.

Sowerby Glass Works (England)

Jain Glass Works (India)

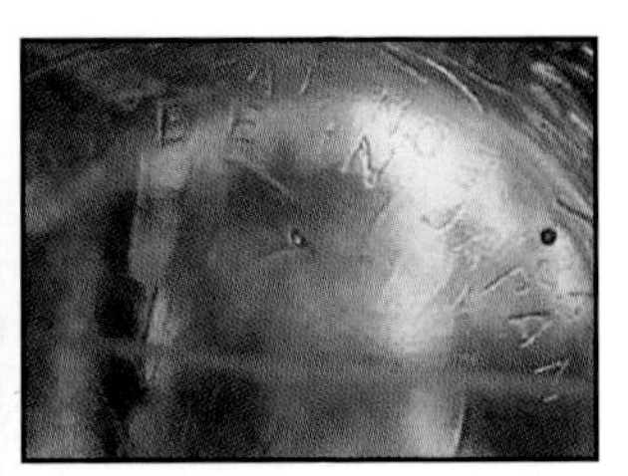

Japanese Trademark on base of Festival Moon tumbler

One of several Czechoslovakian paper labels

Riihimaki Glass Works (Finland)

Paper label on "Jris" Glass following WWII in Germany (U.S. zone)

Made by
Sowerby (England), 1930s

Flower Holder (or Bud Holder)

Marigold	175

Made by
AMV (India), 1930s

Hand Vase

Marigold	225

Made by
Unknown (Argentina), 1930s

Honey Jar w/lid

Marigold	250

Argentina Ribbed Barrel

Made by
Unknown (Argentina?), 1930s

Tumbler

Marigold	125

Also known as
Marguerite

Made by
Brockwitz (Germany), 1920s

Bowl

Marigold	60
Blue	100

Compote

Marigold	90

Rose Bowl

Marigold	200

Vase

Marigold	225

Made by
Austria, 1930s

Bowl, 2 sizes, decorated	
Amethyst or Purple	700
Blue	750
Red	825
Iridized Moonstone	1,350

Bowl in Bride's Basket	
Iridized Moonstone	1,750

Made by
Jain (India), 1930s

Tumbler, very scarce

Marigold	175

Pitcher

Marigold	275

Made by
Crown Crystal (Australia), 1924

Bowl, 5"	
Marigold	170
Amethyst	175

Bowl, 9"	
Marigold	225
Amethyst	450

Made by
Unknown (Argentina), 1930s

Jug, 7¼"
Amber 125

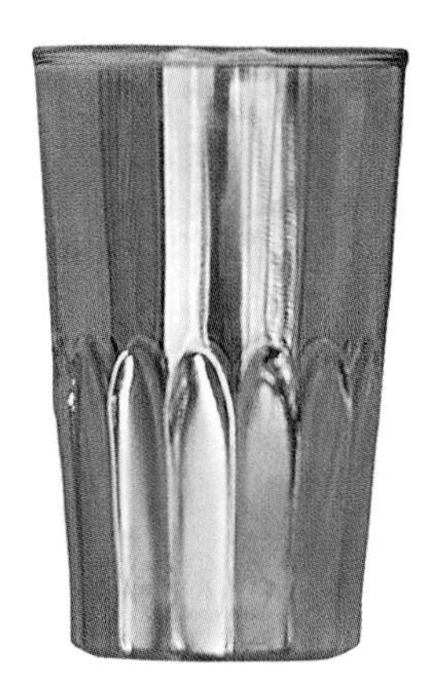

Made by
China, 1930s

Tumbler

Marigold	75

Also known as
Heavy Banded Diamonds

Made by
Crown Crystal (Australia), 1920s

Bowl 5"

Marigold	50
Amethyst	75

Bowl, 9"

Marigold	100
Amethyst	125

Flower set, 2 pcs.

Marigold	150
Amethyst	195

Pitcher, very scarce

Marigold	900
Amethyst	1,250

Tumbler, very scarce

Marigold	250
Amethyst	400

Made by
Inwald (Czechoslovakia), 1930s

Decanter, complete
Marigold 200

Plate
Marigold 200

Tumbler, 2¼"
Marigold 475

Tumbler, 4"
Marigold 450

Made by
Jain (India), 1930s

Pitcher, rare

Marigold	650

Tumbler, rare

Marigold	100

Made by
Rindskopf (Czechoslovakia), 1920s

Juice Tumbler, Ftd.
Marigold 25

Compote
Marigold 40

Goblet
Marigold 25

Made by
Jain (India), 1930s

Tumbler, rare

Marigold	225

Made by
Unknown (Possibly Argentina), 1930s

Decanter

Marigold	175

Wine, stemmed

Marigold	85

Made by
Germany, 1930s

Tumbler

Marigold	75

Also known as
Trailing Berries

Made by
Jain (India), 1930s

Tumbler

Marigold	275

Made by
Jain (India), 1930s

Pitcher, rare	
Marigold	490
Amethyst	560

Tumbler, rare	
Marigold	190
Amethyst	200

Made by
Possibly Sowerby (England), 1920s

Vase, 5½", scarce

Marigold	350

Also known as
Beads & Diamonds

Made by
Leerdam (Holland), 1930s

Compote

Marigold	50
Blue	60

Covered Butter

Marigold	70
Blue	85

Milk Pitcher

Marigold	75
Blue	90

Sugar

Marigold	50
Blue	55

Made by
Cristalerias Rigolleau (Argentina), 1920s

One size, rare	
Marigold	650
Blue	500
Amber	850

Also known as
Dewhirst Berry Band

Made by
Papini (Argentina), 1930s

Carafe, 7"
Marigold 175

Wine
Marigold 75

Decanter
Marigold 200

Tray
Marigold 100

Compote
Marigold 85

Made by
Brockwitz (Germany), 1920s

Bowls	
Marigold	45 – 90
Butter, covered	
Marigold	200
Creamer	
Marigold	35
Sugar, open	
Marigold	30

Made by
Germany, 1940s

Tumbler	
Marigold	250

Made by
Riihimaki (Finland), 1930s

Vase, 8"

Marigold	150
Blue	200

Made by
Unknown, 1930s?

Plate, 6"

Marigold	165

Made by
Crown Crystal (Australia), 1920s

Creamer	
Marigold	40
Pitcher, rare	
Marigold	100
Amethyst	140
Tumbler, rare	
Marigold	75
Amethyst	90

Made by
Unknown (Argentina), 1930s

Pitcher, very scarce

Blue	500

Made by
Brockwitz (Germany), 1930s

Vase	
Marigold	145
Blue	225

Made by
Inwald (Czechoslovakia), 1930s

Bowl, 5"

Marigold	95

Made by
Crown Crystal (Australia), 1920s

Bowl, all shapes

Marigold	90

Made by
Cristalerias Piccardo (Argentina), 1930s

Mug

Marigold	150

Also known as
Butterfly & Christmas Bells

Made by
Crown Crystal (Australia), 1920s

Compote, large	
Marigold	220
Amethyst	245

Made by
Crown Crystal (Australia), 1920s

Compote, large	
Marigold	150
Amethyst	400

Made by
Crown Crystal (Australia), 1920s

Compote, ruffled	
Marigold	175
Black Amethyst	450

Made by
Crown Crystal (Australia), 1920s

Compote	
Marigold	200
Amethyst	400

Made by
Unknown (Norway), 1930s?

Sugar Basket

Marigold	70

Made by
Unknown, 1930s

Bowl, 5½"

Marigold	100

Made by
Jain (India), 1930s

Pitcher	
Marigold	325
Tumbler	
Marigold	125

Made by
Jain (India), 1930s

Tumbler

Marigold	135

Made by
Jain (India), 1930s

Tumber

Marigold	235

Made by
Cristalerias Papini (Argentina), 1930s

Tumbler

Marigold	250

Tumble-up

Marigold	350

Underplate

Marigold	75

Also known as
Sea Thistle

Made by
Sowerby (England), 1920s

Creamer or Sugar

Marigold	45

Rose Bowl

Marigold	125
Blue	75

Made by
Unknown (Finland ?), 1920s

Vase, 4⅞"

Amber	250

Made by
Unknown (Europe), 1930s

Shade

Marigold, each	50

Made by
Unknown (Argentina), 1930s

Ashtray, novelty

Marigold	250

Made by
Brockwitz (Germany), 1930s

Punch Bowl, one piece

Marigold	400

Made by
India, 1930s

Pitcher

Marigold	325

Tumbler

Marigold	135

Made by
CB (India), 1930s

Vase, 6"

Marigold	275

Made by
Jain (India), 1930s

Tumbler

Marigold	225

Made by
Unknown (Europe), 1930s

Compote, large
Marigold 100

Creamer, Stemmed/Open
Marigold 70

Sugar
Marigold 65

Made by
Brockwitz (Germany), 1920s

Compote, large	
Marigold	325
Blue	450

Also known as
Zipper Round

Made by
Unknown, 1930s

Bowl

Marigold	70

Made by
Rindskopf (Czechoslovakia), 1930s

Vase, very scarce

Marigold	325

Made by
Unknown, 1930s

Plate, 7"

Marigold	95

Made by
Paliwal (India), 1930s

Tumbler

Marigold	150

Made by
Rindskopf (Czechoslovakia), 1920s

Powder Jar
Marigold 400

Rose Bowl
Marigold 450

Vase, 7½", very scarce
Marigold 425

Also known as
Chic

Made by
Sowerby (England), 1920s & 1950s

One size	
Marigold	350
Blue	500

Made by
Sowerby (England), 1920s

One size	
Marigold	325
Amethyst	425
Blue	525

Made by
Sowerby (England), 1920s

Creamer

Marigold	75

Sugar, open

Marigold	75

Also known as
Cathedral

Made by
Brockwitz (Germany), Karhula (Finland), EDA (Sweden), 1930s

Bowl, 3½"
Marigold 25

Bowl, 10"
Marigold 50

Bowl, square, 7¾"
Marigold 175

Butterdish, two sizes
Marigold 275

Chalice
Marigold 100
Blue 200

Compote, two sizes
Marigold 60

Creamer, footed
Marigold 60

Epergne, scarce
Marigold 325

Flower Holder
Marigold 135

Pitcher, rare
Blue 3,200

Rose Bowl, scarce
Marigold 200
Blue 400

Vase, 9½", rare
Marigold 325
Amethyst 475
Blue 875

Made by
Riihimaki (Finland), 1930s

Butter	
Amber	300

Made by
Rindskopf (Germany), 1920s

Bowl, 6¼", scarce

Marigold	60

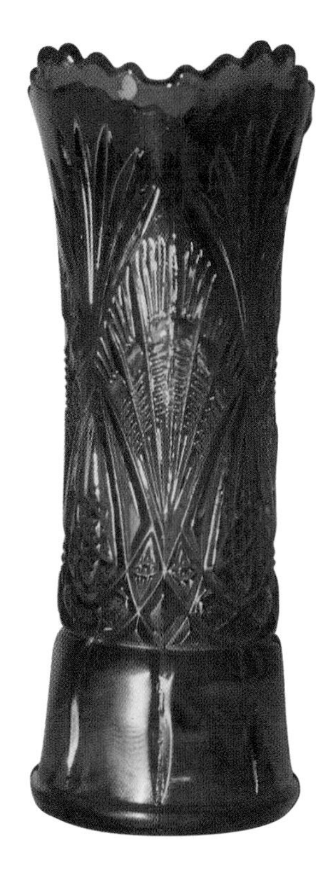

Made by
EDA (Sweden), 1920s

Vase	
Marigold	300
Blue	350

Also known as
Tartan

Made by
Brockwitz (Germany), Riihimaki (Finland), Karhula (Finland), 1930s

Bowl, footed
Marigold 50

Bowl, oval, 12"
Marigold 90

Decanter, rare
Marigold 100

Epergne
Marigold 175

Pitcher, rare
Marigold 1,575

Salver
Marigold 80

Spittoon, rare
Marigold 1,400
Blue 1,275

Vase, scarce
Marigold 175

Wine, very scarce
Marigold 125

Made by
Jain (India), 1930s

Vase

Marigold	225

Also known as
Lady Fingers

Made by
Unknown (Europe), 1930s

Vase, 8"

Marigold	175

Made by
Inwald (Czechoslovakia), 1920s – 30s

Pitcher	
Marigold	550
Tumbler	
Marigold	175

Also known as
Berry Band and Ribs

Made by
Unknown (Argentina), 1930s

Carafe, 7"
Marigold 175

Compote
Marigold 85

Wine
Marigold 75

Decanter
Marigold 200

Tray
Marigold 100

Made by
Jain (India), 1930s

Vase	
Marigold	450

Made by
Jain (India), 1930s

Tumbler

Marigold	225

Made by
Unknown, 1930s?

Bowl, 6¼"

Marigold	60

Made by
Crown Crystal (Australia), 1920s

Banana Bowl	
Marigold	90
Amethyst	115

Bowl, 10"	
Marigold	90
Amethyst	150

Compote	
Marigold	75

Rose Bowl, 9½", rare	
Marigold	175
Amethyst	425

Made by
Brockwitz (Germany), 1930s

Pitcher	
Marigold	475
Tumbler	
Marigold	125

Made by
Unknown, 1930s?

Compote, miniature

Marigold	85

Made by
Jain (India), 1930s

Vase, 5½"

Marigold	70

Made by
Rindskopf (Czechoslovakia), 1920s

Bottle and Stopper	
Marigold	100
Compote (open sugar)	
Marigold	40
Creamer	
Marigold	40
Plate, stemmed	
Marigold	150

Made by
Sowerby (England), 1920s

Bowl, 10⅞"
Marigold 60

Butter
Marigold 90

Compote
Marigold 45

Also known as
Hans

Made by
Sowerby (England), 1920s

Compote

Marigold	150

Bowl

Marigold	70

Creamer

Marigold	55

Made by
Uncertain (Poland ?), 1930s

Bowl, 8"

Marigold	350

Made by
Jain (India), 1930s

Vase	
Marigold	225

Made by
Unknown (Rindskopf ?), 1920s

Bowl, 8 - 9"

Marigold	225

Made by
Sowerby (England), 1920s

Bowl, footed, 7"	
Marigold	225
Amethyst	275
Green	425
Blue	325
Rosebud, scarce	
Marigold	325
Amethyst	475
Whimsey bowl, rare	
Aqua	600

Made by
Inwald (Czechoslovakia), 1920s

Cologne
Marigold 90

Pin Tray
Marigold 60

Puff Box
Marigold 50

Perfume
Marigold 80

Ring Tree
Marigold 85

Tumble-up
Marigold 110

Made by
Unknown, 1930s?

Square Vase

Amethyst	250

Made by
Jain (India), 1930s

Pitcher

Marigold	350

Tumbler

Marigold	165

Made by
Unknown (India), 1930s

Vase	
Marigold	175

Made by
Riihimaki (Finland), or Inwald (Czechoslovakia), or both, 1920s

Pitcher	
Marigold	600
Tumbler	
Marigold	200
Shot Glass	
Marigold	225
Plate	
Marigold	350

Also known as
Queen's Vase

Made by
Rindskopf (Czechoslovakia), 1920s

Vase, 6" – 7½"

Marigold	425

Also known as
Shooting Star

Made by
Brockwitz (Germany)

Butter	
Marigold	150
Compote, 4½"	
Marigold	50
Amethyst	60
Blue	65
Creamer	
Marigold	70
Sugar, open	
Marigold	65

Made by
Jain (India), 1930s
Note: There are two variants.

Vase, 3 sizes

Marigold	300 – 500

Made by
Jain (India), 1930s

Vase	
Marigold	375

Made by
Unknown, 1930s

Vase, 9½"

Marigold	350

Made by
Jain (India), 1920s

Spittoon, (lamp base)
Marigold 450

Tumbler
Marigold 165

Made by
Unknown, 1920s

Vase	
Marigold	400

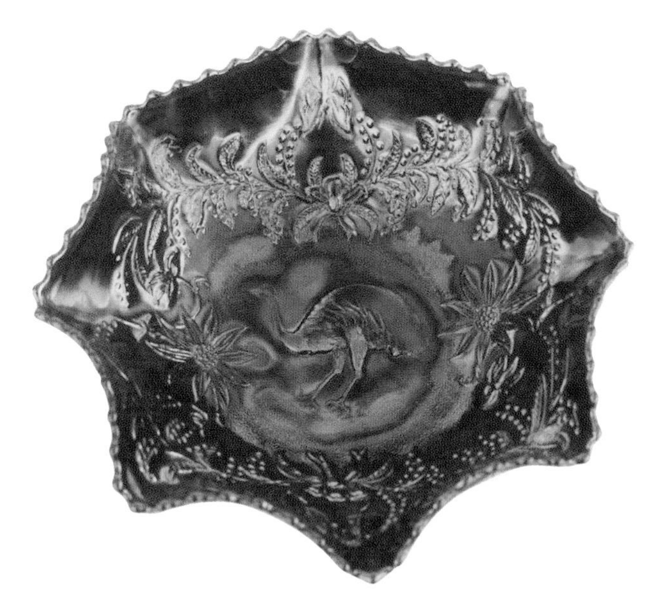

Made by
Crown Crystal (Australia), 1920s

Bowl, 5", rare	
Marigold	150
Amethyst	175

Bowl, 10", rare	
Marigold	900
Amber	1,400
Black Amethyst	1,000

Compote Variant, rare	
Marigold	700
Amethyst	850

Made by
Sowerby (England), 1920s

Compote	
Marigold	70
Lavender	120

Creamer and Sugar	
Marigold	45
Lavender	70

Also known as
Chunky (#2266)

Made by
Sowerby (England), 1920s

Bowl, 7 – 10"

Marigold	60
Amethyst	80
Green	95
Blue	70

Epergne (metal base)

Marigold	125
Blue	145

Made by
Unknown, 1930s?

Plate, rare

Marigold	250

Made by
Unknown (India), 1930s

Pitcher

Marigold	425

Tumbler

Marigold	135

Also known as
Poppy & Hobstar

Made by
Riihimaki (Finland), 1920s

Butter	
Amber	165
Blue	225

Bowl	
Marigold	65
Blue	85

Made by
Riihimaki (Finland), 1930s

Bowl, 8", rare

Marigold	400

Made by
Rindskopf (Czechoslovakia), 1920s

Cracker Jar (metal lid)
Marigold 175

Pitcher
Marigold 300

Tumbler
Marigold 125

Made by
U. S. Glass (Argentina?), 1920s

Jar

Marigold	135

Also known as
Buckingham

Made by
U. S. Glass (Argentina?), 1920s

Jar	
Marigold	165

Also known as
ID KA Chand

Made by
Unknown (Japan), Marked "Made in Japan," 1930s?

Tumbler, rare

Marigold	150

Made by
Unknown, 1920s

Item	Color	Price
Bowl, oval	Marigold	140
Bowl, round	Marigold	135
Butter	Marigold	170
Celery	Marigold	160
Creamer	Marigold	145
Jam Jar with Lid	Marigold	165
Stemmed Cake Stand	Marigold	175
Stemmed Sugar	Marigold	145
Vase	Marigold	150

Made by
Riihimaki (Finland), 1930s

Pitcher

Blue	600

Tumbler

Blue	350

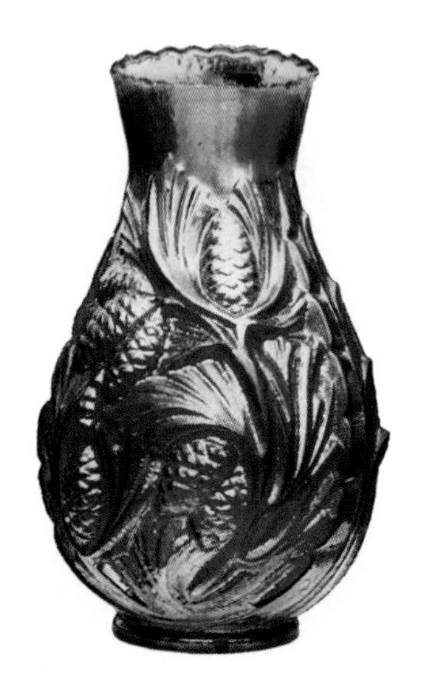

Made by
Unknown (Possibly Coty in France), 1930s?

Vase, 11¾", rare

Marigold	1,500

Made by
Unknown, 1930s?

Novelty Bottle

Marigold	175

Also known as
Goldfish

Made by
Unknown, 1930s?

Bowl, 7½", scarce

Marigold	375

Made by
Jain (India), 1930s

Vase, 2 sizes	
Marigold	100 – 125

Made by
Riihimaki (Finland), 1930s

Tumbler, rare	
Amethyst	325
Blue	275

Pitcher, rare	
Amethyst	950

Made by
Inwald (Czechoslovakia), 1920s

Bowl, 8", rare
Marigold 350

Chop Plate, 12", rare
Marigold 700

Plate, 6¼", rare
Marigold 425

Rose Bowl, rare
Marigold 525

Vase, rare
Marigold 650

Made by
Sowerby (England), 1920s – 30s

Float Boat

Blue	200

Also known as
Daisy Spray

Made by
EDA (Sweden), 1920s

Bowl

Marigold	95
Blue	175

Rose Bowl

Marigold	225
Blue	325

Vase, flared top

Marigold	650
Blue	1,100

Vase, tricorner or turned in top

Marigold	950
Blue	1,500

Also known as
Sugar Cane

Made by
Jain (India), 1930s

Tumbler	
Marigold	175

Made by
Jain (India), 1930s

Vase	
Marigold	200

Also known as
Prism Panels

Made by
Brockwitz (Germany), 1930s

Vase	
Marigold	85
Green	250
Blue	200

Made by
Unknown (Czechoslovakia), 1930s

Atomizer
Marigold 90

Decanter with stopper
Marigold 125

Perfume, 3 sizes
Marigold 80

Pin Box
Marigold 60

Pin Tray, 2 sizes
Marigold 50

Powder Box
Marigold 70

Pitcher, squat
Marigold 175

Tumbler
Marigold 75

Ring Tray
Marigold 70

Wine
Marigold 80

Made by
Riihimaki (Finland), 1920s

Candlesticks, pair	
Pink	250

Made by
EDA (Sweden), Riihimaki (Finland), 1920s – 30s

Bowl, 9" – 11"	
Marigold	70
Amethyst	75
Green	100
Peach Opalescent	200
Amber	225

Bowl on Metal Base, rare	
Lavender	350
Peach Opalescent	300
Teal	350

Plate, 10½", rare	
Amethyst	450
Green	375
Teal	425

Made by
Unknown, 1920s?

Vase, 7½"

Marigold	225

Made by
Sowerby (England), 1920s

Bowl, handle, 5"

Marigold	225

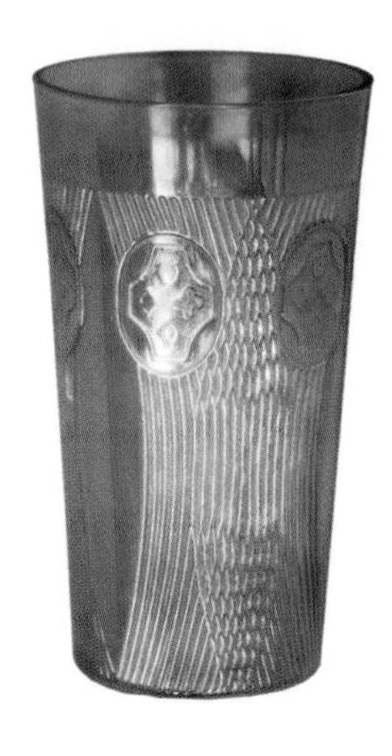

Made by
Jain (India), 1930s

Tumbler

Marigold	175

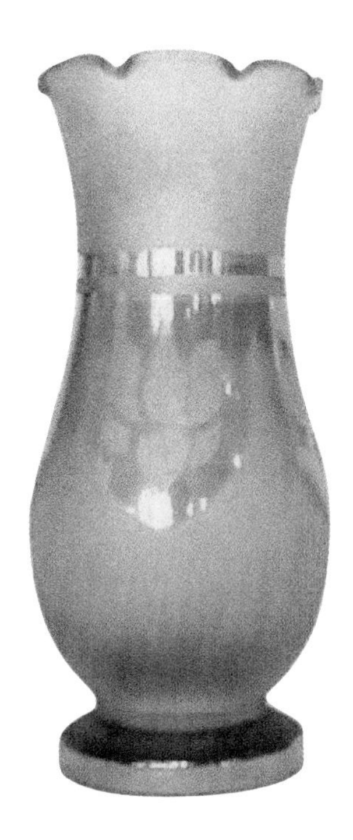

Made by
Jain (India), 1930s

Vase

Marigold	200

Also known as
Fruit Chain

Made by
Unknown (South America), 1930s

Decanter	
Marigold	250
Blue	350
Glass	
Marigold	75
Blue	90

Made by
Unknown, 1930s

Bonboniere with Lid, 5½", very scarce

Marigold	550

Made by
Unknown, 1930s?

Bowl	
Marigold	125

Made by
Cristalerias Papini (Argentina), 1930s

Pitcher
Marigold 350

Tumbler
Marigold 100

Vase
Marigold 145

Made by
Jain (India), 1930s

Tumbler

Marigold	150

Also known as
Monsoon

Made by
Jain (India), 1930s

Pitcher

Marigold	285

Tumbler

Marigold	145

Made by
Jain ? (India), 1930s

Vase, 6½"

Marigold	300

Made by
Jain (India), 1930s

Vase, 8½", rare

Marigold	750

Made by
Questionable (Poland, Finland, Czechoslovakia ?), 1930s

Bowl, 5", rare	
Marigold	225

Made by
India, 1930s

Pitcher

Marigold	350

Also known as
Eureka Cross

Made by
Questionable, 1930s

Tray, 10" x 5½"
Marigold 350

Bowl, 4"
Marigold 175

Bowl, 8"
Marigold 325

Made by
Questionable, 1930s

Bowl, 9"

Marigold	400

Plate, 10"

Marigold	500

Made by
Questionable, 1930s

Tray, rare	
Marigold	350
Bowl	
Marigold	250

Made by
Cristalerias Papini (Argentina), 1928

Ashtray in Tire	
Marigold	225

Also known as
Fantasia

Made by
Cristalerias Piccardo (Argentina), 1934

Pitcher, rare	
Blue	1500
Amber	1700

Tumbler, scarce	
Marigold	450
Blue	325
Amber	700

Also known as

Alexander Floral, Wide Panel Thistle

Made by

Riihimaki (Finland), 1930s

Pitcher, rare	
Blue	700
Amber	750
Tumbler, scarce	
Blue	120
Amber	350

Made by
EDA (Sweden), 1930s

Bowl	
Marigold	165
Blue	235

Rose Bowl	
Marigold	250
Blue	375

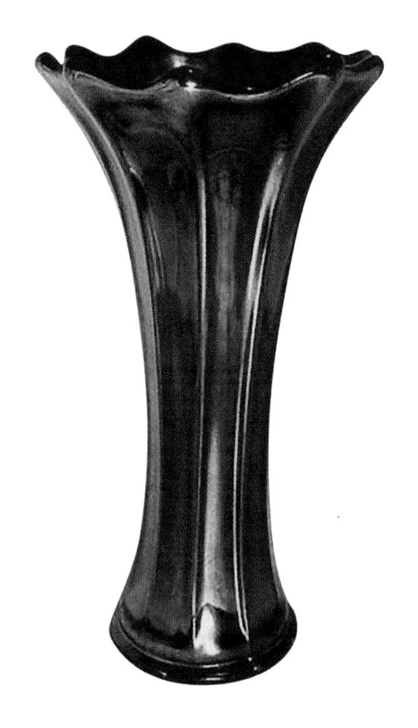

Made by
Crown Crystal (Australia), 1920s

Vase, 8 ribs, very scarce	
Amethyst	375
Black Amethyst	400

Made by
Crown Crystal (Australia), 1920s

Vase, 10 ribs, very scarce

Amethyst	400
Black Amethyst	450

Made by
Uncertain (Czechoslovakia), 1930s

Pitcher, 2 sizes

Marigold	375

Tumbler, 2 sizes

Marigold	50

Spittoon

Marigold	600

Made by
EDA (Sweden), 1925

Jardiniere

Blue	225

Made by
Jain (India), 1930s

One Shape, 5½" – 8"	
Marigold	325
Amethyst	850
Red	1,450

Made by
Jain (India), 1930s

Tumbler

Marigold	180

Made by
Unknown (Possibly England), 1920s

Celery Vase, 6"	
Marigold	85
Amethyst	115
Blue	100

Also known as
Balmoral

Made by
Rindskopf (Czechoslovakia), 1930s

Atomizer
Marigold 85

Cologne
Marigold 90

Lamp
Marigold 250

Powder Box
Marigold 75

Tumbler
Marigold 150

Tumble-up
Marigold 200

Shot Glass
Marigold 80

Made by
Jain (India), 1930s

Vase	
Marigold	190

Made by
Crown Crystal (Australia), 1920s

Compote	
Marigold	85
Amethyst	165
Ice Blue	225

Salver	
Marigold	100
Amethyst	190
Ice Blue	250

Made by
Sowerby (England), 1920s

Bowl

Marigold	30
Amethyst	40
Green	60

Plate

Marigold	70
Amethyst	100
Green	110

Rose Bowl

Marigold	45
Amethyst	55
Green	70

Made by
Karhula (Finland), 1930s

Pitcher	
Marigold	325
Blue	575
Tumbler	
Marigold	125

Made by
Brockwitz (Germany), 1920s

Creamer	
Marigold	45
Sugar, stemmed	
Marigold	45

Made by
Possibly from England, 1920s

Butter	
Marigold	55
Amethyst	75
Blue	70

Frog & Holder	
Marigold	85

Rose Bowl	
Marigold	60
Amethyst	95

Spooner	
Marigold	45

Made by
Unknown (Peru ?), 1930s

Bottle

Marigold	175

Made by
Cristalerias Piccardo (Argentina), 1930s

Pitcher, very scarce

Marigold	400

Made by
Unknown (Peru, Argentina), 1930s

Bottle, scarce

Marigold	175

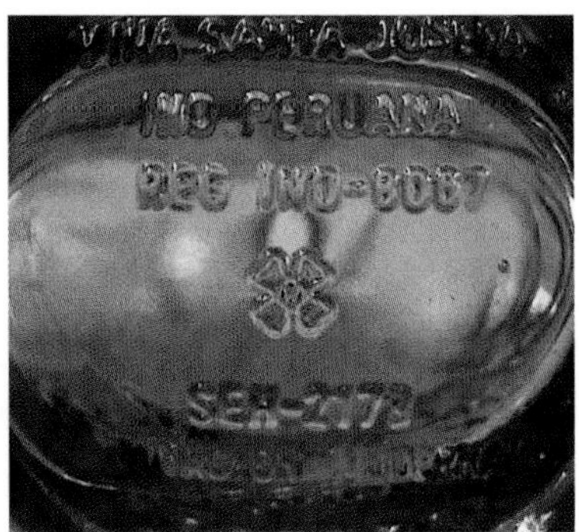

Made by
Unknown (Peru, Argentina), 1930s

Bottle, scarce

Marigold	200

Made by
Unknown, 1930s?

Vase, rare	
Marigold	900
Powder Blue	950

Made by
Jain ? (India), 1930s

Tumbler	
Marigold	140

Made by
Jain (India), 1930s

Pitcher	
Marigold	325

Tumbler	
Marigold	125

Made by
Jain (India), 1930s

Pitcher

Marigold	350

Tumbler

Marigold	100

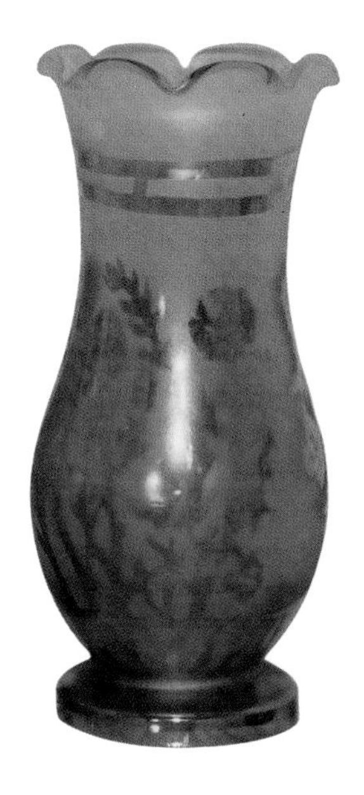

Made by
Jain (India), 1930s

Vase

Marigold	200

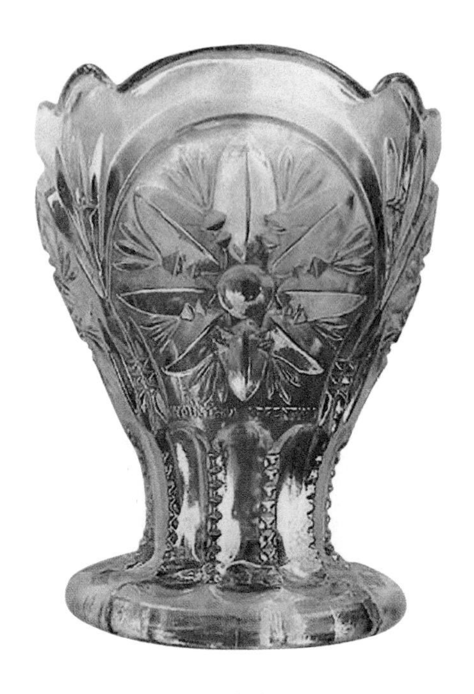

Made by
Cristalerias Papini (Argentina), 1920s

Bowl

Marigold	150

Vase

Marigold	300

Also known as
Inwald's Pinwheel

Made by
Inwald (Czechoslovakia), 1930s

Tumbler, rare

Marigold	600

Also known as
Diamond Vane

Made by
Rindskopf (Czechoslovakia), 1920s – 30s

Creamer

Marigold	70

Sugar, open

Marigold	60

Made by
Inwald (Czechoslovakia), 1920s

Bowl (Jardineire)

Blue	400

Vase

Marigold	475

Made by
Inwald (Czechoslovakia), 1920s

Bowls, various shapes
Marigold 60+

Decanter
Marigold 200

Juice Tumbler
Marigold 125

Miniature Tumbler
Marigold 150

Pitcher
Marigold 325

Tumbler
Marigold 90

Wine
Marigold 40

Made by
Cristalerias Piccardo (Argentina), 1930s

Vase, 8", rare	
Amethyst	375

Also known as
Acanthus

Made by
Inwald (Czechoslovakia), 1930s

Vase, 6"

Marigold	600

Made by
Uncertain (India), 1930s

Water Jar	
Marigold	250

Made by
Uncertain (India), 1930s

Water Jar	
Marigold	250

Made by
Crown Crystal (Australia), 1920s

Bowl, 5"

Marigold	100
Amethyst	180

Bowl, 9½"

Marigold	300
Amethyst	500

Also known as
Fantasy Flower

Made by
Jain (India), 1930s

Tumbler

Marigold	165

Made by
Uncertain (India), 1930s

Vase

Marigold	200

Made by
Crown Crystal (Australia), 1920s

Bowl, 5"	
Marigold	95
Amethyst	185

Bowl, 9½"	
Marigold	225
Amethyst	325

Made by
Crown Crystal (Australia), 1920s

Jardiniere, from large bowl, very rare	
Amethyst	800

Bowl, 5"	
Marigold	95
Amethyst	185

Bowl, 9"	
Marigold	225
Amethyst	325

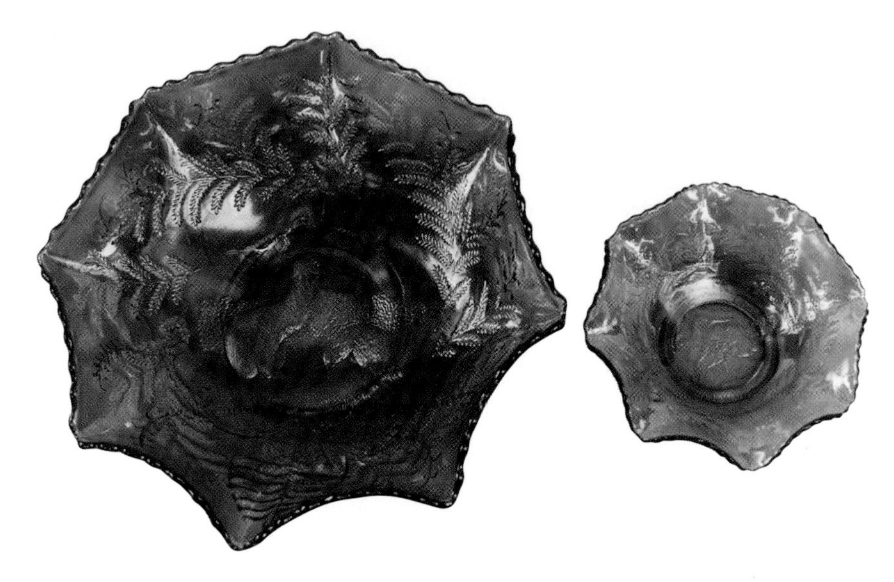

Made by
Crown Crystal (Australia), 1920s

Bowl, 5", rare

Marigold	250
Amethyst	200

Bowl, 10", rare

Marigold	350
Amethyst	1000

Made by
Sowerby (England), 1920s

Bowl, 8"
Marigold 55

Rose Bowl, footed
Marigold 75

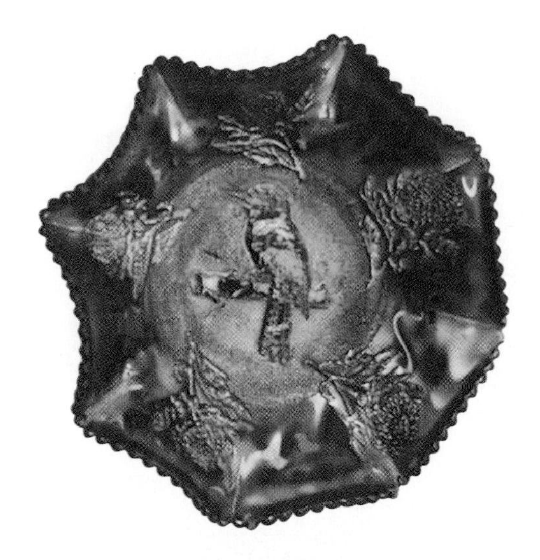

Made by
Crown Crystal (Australia), 1920s

Bowl, 5"	
Marigold	175
Amethyst	225
Black Amethyst	165

Bowl, 9"	
Marigold	425
Amethyst	1,300

Bowl, 9", lettered, very rare	
Marigold	1,500

Made by
Crown Crystal (Australia), 1920s

Bowl, 12", Whimsey, very rare

Black Amethyst	2,700

Made by
EDA (Sweden), 1930s

Vase, 6" – 12", very scarce	
Marigold	1,350
Amethyst	4,500
Blue	2,500
Teal	3,000

Made by
Crown Crystal (Australia), 1920s

Bowl, 7" – 8"	
Marigold	100
Amethyst	145

Made by
Sowerby (England), 1920s

Bowl, footed	
Marigold	40
Creamer, footed	
Marigold	45
Amethyst	50
Pickle Dish, handle	
Marigold	45

Made by
Crown Crystal (Australia), 1920s

Bowl	
Marigold	115

Made by
Sowerby (England), 1920s

Bowl, 7"

Marigold	55

Made by
Sowerby (England), 1920s

Creamer, footed

Marigold	50

Made by
Jain (India), 1930s

Vase	
Marigold	195

Also known as
Prosperity

Made by
Indiana, then a non-American company

Pitcher, rare	
Marigold	1,200
Blue	1,000

Tumbler, rare	
Marigold	450
Blue	250

Made by
Cristalerias Piccardo (Argentina), 1930s

Plate	
Marigold	225

Made by
Jain (India), 1930s

Pitcher	
Marigold	350

Tumbler	
Marigold	95

Made by
Jain (India), 1930s

Tumbler

Marigold	150

Made by
Crown Crystal (Australia), 1920s

Bowl, 5"

Marigold	95
Amethyst	200

Bowl, 8" – 10"

Marigold	250
Amethyst	475

Made by
Jain (India), 1930s

Shot Glass, rare
Marigold 175

Made by
Molineaux, Webb (England), 1926

Flower Holder with Frog

Amber	100

Made by
Uncertain, 1930s?

Basket, Handled, large

Marigold	65

Made by
Rindskopf (Czechoslovakia), 1920s

Vase

Marigold	260

Made by
Uncertain (Probably Rindskopf), 1920s

Compote, 7½"

Marigold	160

Also known as
Diamond Point

Made by
Possibly Brockwitz (Germany), 1920s

Basket, 7½"

Marigold	40
Green	95

Bowl, 9", rare

Green	160

Made by
Cristales Mexicanos (Mexico), 1930s

Vase, footed, 8"	
Marigold	90

Also known as
Greta

Made by
Leerdam (Holland), 1920s

Butter
Marigold 135

Cake Stand
Marigold 95

Compote
Marigold 75

Made by
Brockwitz (Germany), 1930s

Cordial Set, rare	
Marigold	1,250

Water Set	
Marigold	900

Made by
Jain (India), 1930s

Tumbler, rare
Marigold 290

Made by
Jain (India), 1930s

Tumbler, rare

Marigold	325

Made by
Jain (India), 1930s

Vase	
Marigold	250

Made by
Probably Sowerby (England), 1920s

Bowl, 4½"

Marigold	25
Blue	30

Bowl, shallow, 8½"

Marigold	40
Blue	45

Rose Bowl, whimsey

Marigold	95

Made by
EDA (Sweden), 1920s

Bowl	
Marigold	210
Blue	325

Rose Bowl	
Marigold	350
Blue	500

Made by
Unknown, 1930s?

Pitcher

Marigold	450

Also known as
Globus

Made by
Brockwitz (Germany), 1920s

Banana Boat, rare
Marigold 135

Bowl, 8½"
Marigold 45

Bowl, 14"
Marigold 80

Butter
Marigold 100

Candlesticks, each, rare
Marigold 90

Cheese Keeper, rare
Marigold 175

Compote
Marigold 55

Cordial
Marigold 35

Creamer
Marigold 40

Decanter with Stopper
Marigold 250

Jar with Lid
Marigold 65

Pitcher, squat, scarce
Marigold 225

Sugar, stemmed
Marigold 50

Tray
Marigold 75

Vase, very scarce
Marigold 400

Made by
EDA (Sweden), 1930s

Jardiniere	
Marigold	325
Blue	500

Vase	
Marigold	350
Blue	575

Made by
Brockwitz (Germany), 1930s

Bowl, 2 sizes

Marigold	100 – 150
Blue	175 – 200

Rose Bowl, 2 sizes

Marigold	225 – 275
Blue	300 – 400

Also known as
London

Made by
Brockwitz (Germany), 1920s

Butter	
Marigold	125
Creamer	
Marigold	55
Sugar, open	
Marigold	55

Made by
Cristales Mexicanos (Mexico), 1930s

Decanter
Marigold 850

Tumbler, rare
Marigold 500

Made by
Uncertain (First U.S. Glass, then possibly Argentina), 1930s

Pitcher, very rare

Marigold	700

Tumbler, rare

Marigold	200
Green	400
Blue	550

Pitcher, whimsey, no spout

Green	1,200

Made by
Uncertian (India), 1930s

Vase, 9"

Marigold	180
Blue	325

Made by
Unknown (Found in Malaysia), 1930s?

Bowl, 5½"

Marigold	60

Also known as
Cane Panels

Made by
Rindskopf (Czechoslovakia), 1920s

Vase, 8"

Marigold	250

Made by
Crown Crystal (Australia), 1920s

Bowl, 9¾"

Marigold	1,500

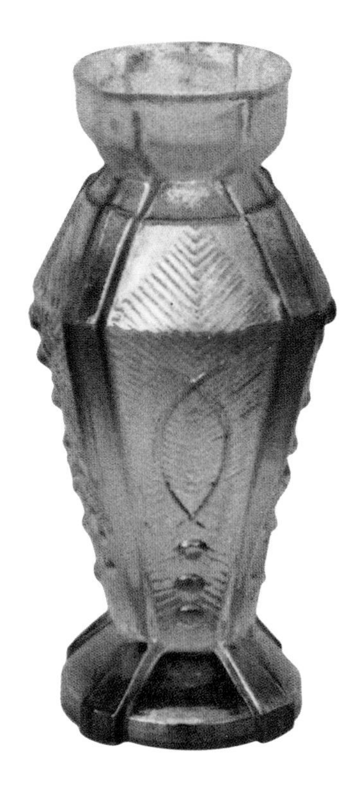

Made by
Unknown (India), 1930s

Vase, 5½"

Marigold	150

Also known as
Block Diamond

Made by
Unknown, 1920s?

Jam Jar with Lid

Marigold	55

Also known as
Nola

Made by
Inwald (Czechoslovakia), 1920s

Tumbler

Marigold	90

Pitcher

Marigold	325

Decanter

Marigold	250

Made by
Riihimaki (Finland), 1920s

Bowl

Marigold	70

Made by
Jain ? (India), 1930s

Vase, 8½"

Marigold	225

Made by
Inwald (Czechoslovakia), 1920s

Candlesticks, pair

Marigold	80

Made by
Cristalieria Papini? Riihimaki? (Both show it in catalogs), 1920s – 30s

Compote
Marigold 250

Pitcher
Marigold 375

Tumbler
Marigold 75

Made by
Unknown, 1930s?

Candlesticks, pair

Marigold	400

Also known as
Mayuri

Made by
Unknown (India), 1930s

Vase, 6"

Marigold	165

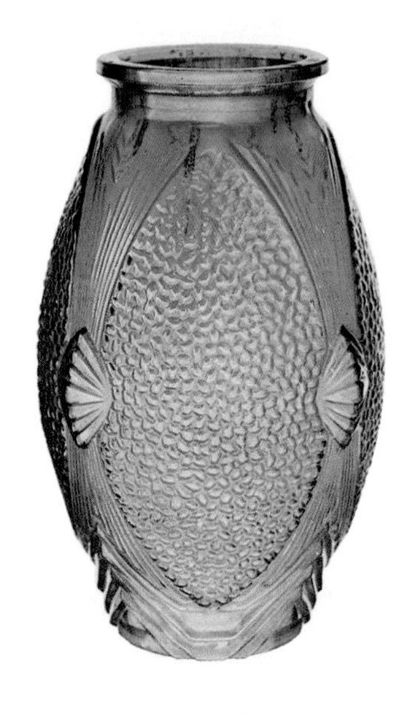

Made by
Unknown, 1930s?

Vase, 11¼", rare

Blue	750
Amber	700

Made by
Unknown (Czechoslovakia), 1930s?

Sugar Bowl

Marigold	45

Made by
Sowerby (England), 1920s

Bowl, 4"

Marigold	40

Bowl, 7"

Marigold	60
Amethyst	70
Blue	70

Butter

Marigold	85

Compote

Marigold	50
Amethyst	70
Blue	60

Creamer

Marigold	75
Amethyst	100
Aqua	100

Rose Bowl

Marigold	250

Sugar, stemmed or flat

Marigold	75

Made by
U.S. Glass, 1907; Argentina, 1930s

Tumble-up Set, 3 pieces

Marigold	450
Blue	600

Wine Set, Complete, 8 pieces

Marigold	575

Made by
Rindskopf ? Unknown at this time, 1920s?

Oval Bowl, 8"

Marigold	60

Made by
Jain (India), 1930s

Tumbler	
Marigold	200
Vase	
Marigold	350
Blue	500

Made by
Crown Crystal (Australia), 1920s

Bowl, 4" – 6", rare

Marigold	95
Amethyst	175

Bowl, 7" – 8¼", rare

Marigold	200
Amethyst	450

Made by
Sowerby (England), 1920s

Bowl, 8", rare

Marigold	125

Vase, 6½"

Marigold	350
Amethyst	450

Vase, 8"

Marigold	200
Amethyst	375
Blue	450

Made by
Unknown, 1920s?

Bowl	
Marigold	55
Rose Bowl	
Marigold	95

Made by
Brockwitz ?, 1930s

Pitcher

Marigold	425

Tumbler, scarce

Marigold	150

Goblet

Marigold	90

Made by
Cristalerias Piccardo (Argentina), 1920s

Covered Candy Dish

Amber	250

Also known as
Coronet

Made by
Inwald (Czechoslovakia), 1920s

Vase, 10½", rare

Marigold	750

Also known as
Duchesse

Made by
Uncertain, possibly Brockwitz (Germany), 1930s

Basket, handled
Marigold 150

Made by
Uncertain (Malaysia?), 1920s

Bowl, 8½"

Marigold	45

Rose Bowl

Marigold	70

Made by
Unknown (Germany), 1930s

Cordial Set (Decanter, Tray) Complete

Marigold	475

Shot Glass, 2¼"

Marigold	75

Made by
Jain (India), 1930s

Tumbler

Marigold	135

Also known as
Bars and Cross Box

Made by
Rindskopf, 1930s

Pitcher, rare

Marigold	800

Tumbler

Marigold	150

Made by
Unknown, 1920s?

Butter	
Marigold	125

Creamer, or Sugar, each	
Marigold	60

Made by
Uncertain (possibly EDA of Sweden), 1930s

Bowl

Marigold	150

Made by
Unknown, 1930s?

Jardiniere	
Marigold	275

Made by
Brockwitz (Germany), 1920s

Cordial
Marigold 200

Decanter with Stopper
Marigold 600

Goblet
Marigold 200

Pitcher
Marigold 650

Tray
Marigold 300

Tumbler, very rare
Marigold 1,500

Clock, rare
Marigold 700

Made by
Unknown (Germany), 1940s?

Tumbler

Marigold	300

Also known as
Diamond Wedges

Made by
EDA (Sweden), 1920s

Vase, rare

Blue	425

Bowl, scarce

Blue	225

Made by
EDA (Sweden), 1920s

Vase	
Marigold	275
Blue	550

Made by
NCP Cristalerias Papini (Argentina), 1930s

Tumbler	
Marigold	65

Made by
Sowerby (England), 1920s?

Sugar, open

Marigold	55

Made by
Unknown (Belgium ?), 1930s?

Cake Stand, very scarce

Amber	425

Made by
Riihimaki (Finland), 1930s?

Pitcher, rare

Blue	950

Tumbler, rare

Blue	450

Milk Pitcher, rare

Blue	625

Made by
Riihimaki (Finland), 1930s

Tumbler	
Blue	225

Made by
Unknown (Inwald ?, Rindskopf ?), 1930s?

Vase, 6" – 10"
Marigold 150 – 400

Made by

Unknown (U.S. Glass originally made this pattern but Carnival pieces are believed to be from South America), 1920s?

Bowl, small, sauce

Marigold	35

Butter Dish

Marigold	400

Creamer

Marigold	75

Juice Tumbler, rare

Marigold	150

Pitcher, 2 shapes, very scarce

Marigold	325
Blue	1,400

Pitcher, squat, rare

Marigold	600

Tumbler, scarce

Marigold	135
Blue	350

Sugar

Marigold	95

Tray, rare

Marigold	300
Blue	500

Also known as
Ariadne

Made by
Brockwitz (Germany), 1930s

Tumbler, rare

Marigold	700

Made by
Both Brockwitz (Germany) and EDA (Sweden), 1930s

Bowl, 6", scarce

Marigold	105
Amethyst	175
Blue	140

Bowl, 8¼"

Marigold	150
Amethyst	350
Blue	225

Butter, rare

Marigold	450
Blue	600

Pitcher, rare

Marigold	1,150
Blue	1,700

Rose Bowl, small, very scarce

Marigold	1,600

Rose Bowl, large, very scarce

Blue	1,600

Vase, round, rare

Marigold	500
Blue	900

Vase, small, scarce

Marigold	800
Blue	1,500

Vase, medium, scarce

Marigold	1,100
Blue	2,000

Vase, large, scarce

Marigold	1,300
Blue	4,000

Made by
Uncertain, possibly EDA, 1920s

Compote, large	
Marigold	175

Made by
Unknown, 1930s?

Jar with Lid

Marigold	100

Made by
Unknown (Argentina), 1930s

Mini Loving Cup

Marigold	195

Made by
Uncertain (England), 1930s

Vase

Marigold	80

Made by
Sowerby (England), 1920s

Vase, rare	
Marigold	1,500
Amethyst	2,000

Made by
Sowerby (England), 1920s

Ashtray, handled, 5"

Marigold	45
Amethyst	60

Plate, 7"

Marigold	165

Made by
Jain, AMV (India), 1930s

Vase, rare	
Marigold	1,000

Made by
Jain (India), 1930s

Pitcher

Marigold	425

Tumbler

Marigold	100

Made by
Uncertain (India), 1930s

Tumbler

Marigold	150

Also known as
Radiant Daisy

Made by
U.S. Glass in 1918, Iittala (Finland) in 1920s, 1918 – 1920s

Bowl, 8" – 9"
Blue 165

Punch Cup
Green Slag 75

Made by
Jain (India), 1930s

Tumbler, very scarce

Marigold	225

Made by
Sowerby (England), Questionable (after 1930)

Swan	
Amethyst	350

Made by
Jain (India), 1930s

Pitcher

Marigold	350

Tumbler

Marigold	90

Made by
Jain (India), 1930s

Pitcher

Marigold	365

Tumbler

Marigold	100

Made by
Unknown (Sowerby ?), 1920s?

Bowl, 8", scarce

Marigold	40

Bowl, 5", scarce

Marigold	25

Butter, very scarce

Marigold	85

Compote

Marigold	55

Creamer, small

Marigold	25

Sugar, open, scarce

Marigold	30

Also known as
Column Flower

Made by
Brockwitz (Germany) then Riihimaki (Finland), 1920s, 1930s

Vase, rare	
Marigold	900
Blue	750

Made by
Crown Crystal (Australia), 1920s

Pitcher

Marigold	350

Made by
Unknown, 1930s?

Decanter, 4 stemmed cordials and tray

Marigold	1,500

Made by
Riihimaki (Finland), 1930s

Vase, 10½", scarce

Marigold	350
Blue	450

Made by
Sowerby (England), 1920s

Sauce, 4 handles

Marigold	95

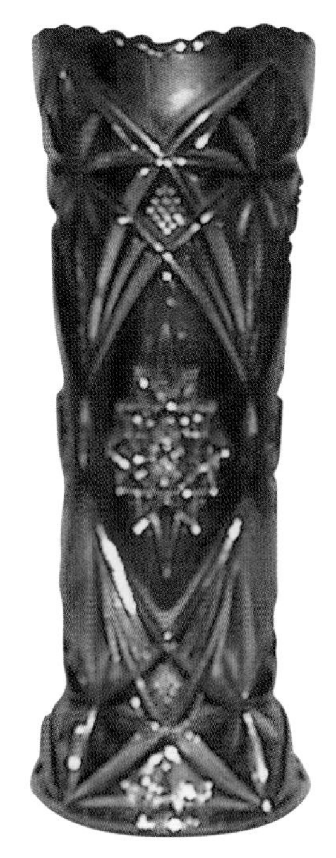

Made by
Riihimaki ? (Finland), 1930s

Vase, 7¾"	
Marigold	85
Blue	145

Made by
Unknown, 1930s?

Bowl, 7" – 9", scarce
Marigold 65

Made by
Rindskopf (Czechoslovakia), 1920s

Compote
Marigold 45

Creamer
Marigold 75

Made by
EDA (Sweden), 1931

Vase, 2 sizes	
Marigold	300
Blue	500

Made by
Brockwitz (Germany), 1930s

Bowl, 9", rare

Marigold	300

Also known as
Amerika

Made by
U.S. Glass (1915), EDA (Sweden, 1925), Riihimaki (Finland, 1930s)

Bowl	
Marigold	225
Amethyst	375
Blue	275

Rose Bowl, 3 sizes, rare	
Marigold	350
Amethyst	150
Blue	500

Also known as
Zurich

Made by
Brockwitz (Germany), 1920s

Jardiniere	
Marigold	250
Blue	295

*This was actually part of the Curved Star line.

Made by
Brockwitz (Germany), 1920s
EDA (Sweden), 1930s
Karhula (Finland), 1930s

Bowls, various

Marigold	75 – 100
Blue	100 – 145

Plate, 6"

Blue	275

Rose Bowl, small, 5½"

Marigold	100
Blue	175

Rose Bowl, large, 8"

Marigold	175
Amethyst	325
Blue	300

Trays, various

Marigold	45 – 85
Blue	60 – 100

Vase

Marigold	85
Blue	145

Made by
Crown Crystal (Australia), 1920s

Vase	
Black Amethyst	500

Made by
Riihimaki (Finland), 1920s

Vase

Marigold	425
Blue	500
Amber	600

Vase, whimsey, small

Blue	700

Made by
Brockwitz (Germany), 1920s

Giant Tumbler (Vase)	
Marigold	625
Blue	500

*Not really a tumbler but a vase and actually part of the Northern Lights pattern.

Made by
Unknown (England ?), 1920s

Bowl, footed, 6"
Marigold 50

Creamer or Sugar, each
Marigold 60

Nut Bowl
Marigold 75

Plate/Low Bowl, footed, 8½"
Marigold 100

Made by
Sowerby (England), 1920s

Bowl, 6", rare

Marigold	200

Made by
Cristalerias Papini (Argentina), 1930s

Tumble-up, 3 pieces

Marigold	175

Made by
EDA (Sweden), 1920s – 30s

Bowl, footed, 8"

Marigold	175
Blue	300

Also known as
Piping Shrike

Made by
Crown Crystal (Australia), 1920s

Bowl, 5"	
Marigold	165
Amethyst	180

Bowl, 9½"	
Marigold	350
Amethyst	600
Aqua	1,200

Made by
Sowerby (England), 1920s

Butter

Marigold	245

Creamer

Vaseline	125

Made by
EDA (Sweden), 1920s

Bowl

Blue	225

Vase, 7½"

Blue	350

Made by
Crown Crystal (Australia), 1928

Bowl, 7"

Marigold	175

Also known as
Niobe

Made by
Brockwitz (Germany), 1929 – 1931

Butter
Marigold 65

Celery Vase
Marigold 55

Compote, small, scarce
Marigold 75

Creamer, Sugar or Spooner
Marigold 50

Made by
Uncertain (India), 1930s

Vase	
Marigold	175

Made by
Brockwitz (Germany), 1920s

Biscuit Jar

Marigold	200
Blue	350

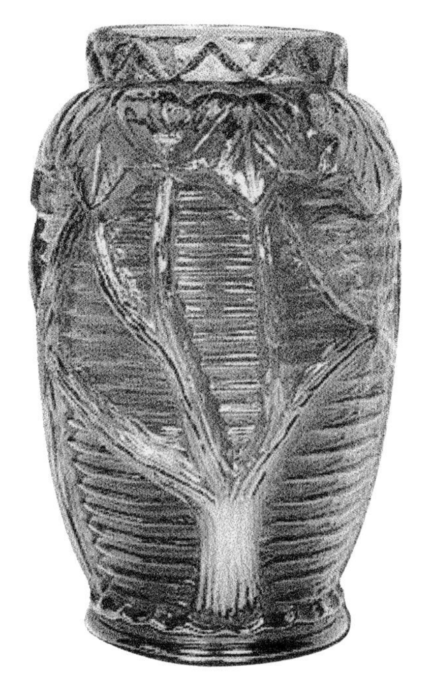

Made by
Uncertain, 1930s?

Vase, rare	
Marigold	1,600

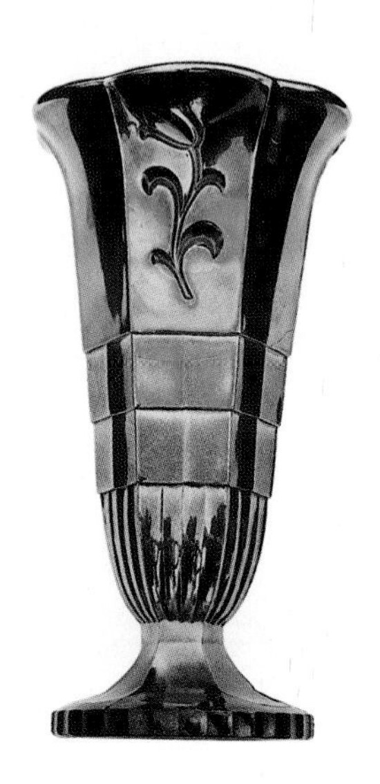

Made by
EDA (Sweden), 1920s

Vase	
Marigold	125
Black Amethyst	325
Blue	325

Also known as
Australian Grape

Made by
Jain (India), 1930s

Tumbler, 5½"

Marigold	250

Made by
Unknown (Argentina), 1930s?

Decanter

Marigold	150

Made by
Unknown (Argentina)

Rose Bowl	
Marigold	250
Lady's Spittoon	
Marigold	350
Bud Vase	
Marigold	225

Made by
EDA (Sweden), 1920s

Banana Boat (Jardiniere)	
Marigold	175
Amethyst	325

Made by
Cristales Mexicanos (Mexico), 1930s

Candle Vase, 4½", rare

Marigold	450

Made by
Crown Crystal (Australia), 1930s

Bowl, 9"	
Marigold	150
Amethyst	185

Made by
Unknown, 1930s

Vase, 12½"

Marigold	250

Made by
Riihimaki (Finland), 1920s

Cider Pitcher	
Blue	350

Tumbler, rare	
Marigold	340
Blue	250
Amber	225

Tumbler, whimsey, rare	
Marigold	300

Vase, rare	
Marigold	325

Made by
Riihimaki (Finland)

Compote	
Marigold	100
Amber	150
Smoky Blue	175

Bowl, Small Berry	
Marigold	35
Blue	50
Pink	40

Bowl, Large Berry	
Marigold	70
Pink	100

Plate, Chop	
Marigold	250
Blue	350

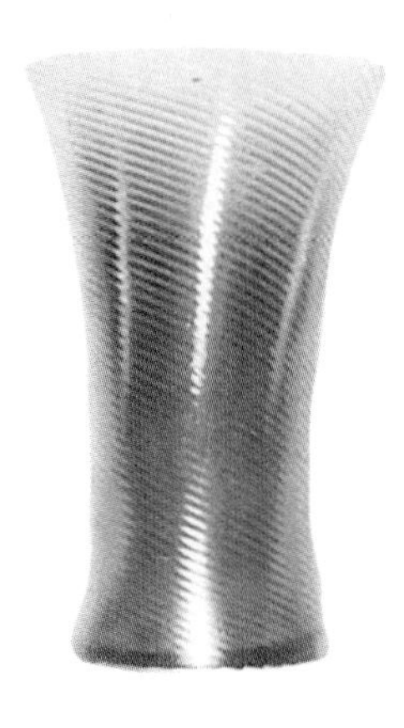

Made by
Jain (India), 1930s

Tumbler (2 sizes, 2 shapes)

Marigold	275

Made by
Sowerby (England), 1920s

Bowl with Base, complete	
Marigold	250
Amethyst	400

Made by
Uncertain, 1930s?

Vase, 6¼"	
Marigold	150
Black Amethyst	200

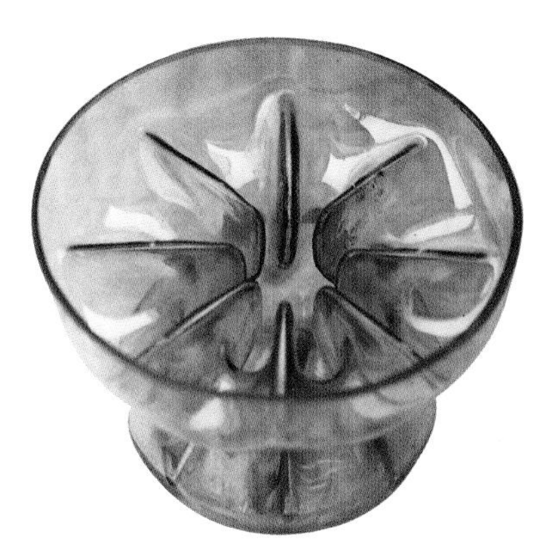
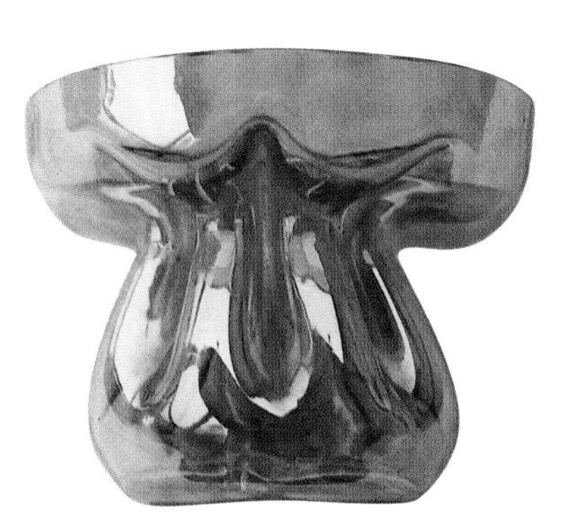

Made by
Unknown (Czechoslovakia), 1930s

Flower Arranger, rare	
Marigold	150
Ice Blue	95

Made by
Uncertain (Argentina ?, Czechoslovakia?), 1930s(?)

Bowl, 10", oval

Marigold	125

Cordial Set, Tray, Decanter & 4 Cordials, Complete

Marigold	1,400

Other Titles by Bill Edwards & Mike Carwile

Standard Encyclopedia of Carnival Glass 10th Edition

This edition introduces almost 100 new patterns and almost 200 new photographs, bringing the total to over 2,000 color patterns. Grading information and salesmen's samples are included, as well as a section on hatpins. All pieces and patterns are described in detail with important facts, colors, histories, and sizes. The bound-in price guide includes virtually every piece of carnival glass. A multitude of companies are represented, including Dugan, Fenton, Imperial, Northwood, Cambridge, Westmoreland, Fostoria, Heisey, McKee, Jeannette, and the U.S. Glass Company. There is also a new illustrated section on Millersburg Peacock patterns, as well as one on company trademarks. 2006 values.

Item #6925 • ISBN: 1-57432-486-1 • 8½ x 11
384 Pgs. • HB • $29.95

Standard Encyclopedia of Carnival Glass Price Guide, 15th Edition

This price guide is bound into the *Standard Encyclopedia of Carnival Glass, Tenth Edition*, but is also offered separately. The fifteenth edition is crammed with new additions, with virtually every known piece of carnival glass evaluated. Listed alphabetically by pattern name are over 25,000 prices for this glass, as well as updated values, company names, and sizes. All prices listed are based on extensive research of auction sales, shop taggings, and private sales. 2006 values.

Item #6926 • ISBN: 1-57432-487-X • 8½ x 11
96 Pgs. • PB • $9.95

Standard Encyclopedia of PRESSED GLASS

4th Edition, 1860 – 1930

This all-new collector's encyclopedia features approximately 135 new patterns and photographs, bringing the total to more than 1,600 photos showcasing the exquisite patterns and beautiful colors of the quality pressed glass produced for 60 years in America. Bill Edwards and Mike Carwile are authorities on pressed, carnival, and opalescent glass, and the sales of their other three editions of *Standard Encyclopedia of Pressed Glass* prompted this fourth edition. 2005 values.

Item #6644 • ISBN: 1-57432-452-7 • 8½ x 11 • 432 Pgs. • HB • $29.95

Standard Encyclopedia of OPALESCENT GLASS

5th Edition

Glass production by both American and English glass companies from 1880 to 1930 is covered in this new edition. With around 130 new patterns featured, this expanded volume now holds over 850 color photographs. Detailed information on several prominent glass manufacturers is again included, and the attached price guide has been enlarged to include nearly 6,400 pieces in six different colors. A new feature of the price guide is the addition of values for the "after 1930" section of the book, not priced in previous editions. 2005 values.

Item #6566 • ISBN: 1-57432-424-1 • 8½ x 11 • 272 Pgs. • HB • $29.95

Standard Encyclopedia of MILLERSBURG CRYSTAL

This book is filled with almost 200 photos, including opalescent, frosted, gilded, ruby and lime stained, and maiden blush stained. An extensive history of the factory filled with old advertisements and factory and employee photos are highlights. Also featured are Butler Brothers catalogs and Jefferson's Canadian Glass Factory catalogs from Ontario. 2001 values.

Item #5832 • ISBN: 1-57432-225-7 • 8½ x 11 • 144 Pgs. • HB • $24.95